Will Th͏̶ ͏?)

W.C.C.
MINETY C.E. SCHOOL
SAWYERS HILL,
MINETY,
MALMESBURY, WILTS
SN16 9
TEL: 0666

"Will this fit?" Fred asks

Mum.

"That will not fit," Mum says.

"And this, will it fit?" Fred

thinks.

"That will not fit," says Mum.

Mum gets a big, red cloth.

"This will fit," she says.

"This is the best!" says Fred.

Game page

On the next page is a game to help the pupil practise reading words at this level.

Photocopy the page two, three or four times (depending on the number of players) onto card.

Cut the cards out and play snap.

Encourage the reader to say the sounds in the word and blend the sounds together fast throughout the word. The teacher/parent should model this phonic approach whilst playing the game.